Reading My Bible in SUMMER

LOU HEATH and BETH TAYLOR

BROADMAN PRESS
Nashville, Tennessee

To our grandchildren
with love and prayers

© Copyright 1986 • Broadman Press
All rights reserved
4243-21
ISBN: 0-8054-4321-5
Dewey Decimal Classification: J242
Subject Heading: MEDITATIONS
Library of Congress Catalog Card Number: 86-20628
Printed in the United States of America

Unless otherwise noted, Scripture quotations are from the King James Version of the Bible.
Scripture quotations marked (GNB) are from the *Good News Bible*, the Bible in Today's English Version. Old Testament: Copyright © American Bible Society 1976; New Testament: Copyright © American Bible Society 1966, 1971, 1976. Used by permission.
Scripture quotations marked (NASB) are from the *New American Standard Bible*. Copyright © The Lockman Foundation, 1960, 1962, 1963, 1968, 1971, 1972, 1973, 1975, 1977. Used by permission.
Scripture quotations marked (NIV) are from the HOLY BIBLE *New International Version*, copyright © 1978, New York Bible Society. Used by permission.

Library of Congress Cataloging-in-Publication Data

Heath, Lou Mishler.
  Reading my Bible in the summer.

  Summary: A collection of daily devotional readings
for the summer season, including Bible stories and
verses, modern examples, questions, and suggested
activities.
    1. Children—Prayer-books and devotions—English.
2. Bible—Children's use. [1. Prayer books and
devotions. 2. Christian life] I. Taylor, Beth.
II. Title.
BV4870.H387   1987   242'.62   86-20628
0-8054-4321-5 (pbk.)

Dear Boys and Girls,

We have written this book especially for you. We hope you will begin to read your Bible every day. The Bible is God's Word to you. It will help you know how God wants you to live and be happy.

Choose a special time of the day to read your Bible. Choose a quiet place to read your Bible.

Each page in this book lists a Bible passage to read. Some pages have puzzles or questions for you to think about and to do. Close this time with prayer.

Your Friends,

Mrs. Lou

Mrs. Beth

Decisions

July 1

Read the Bible:

Locate in your Bible and lightly color Philippians 2:14 and Leviticus 19:18.

"Do everything without complaining or arguing" (Philippians 2:14, GNB).

"Do not take revenge on anyone or continue to hate him, but love your neighbor as you love yourself. I am the Lord" (Leviticus 19:18, GNB).

Think About This:

Have you ever noticed that some people complain about almost everything? Complaining and grumbling can become a bad habit. Holding grudges—staying angry and not forgiving someone—can cause many problems. You can decide to think before you speak. You can decide to quit complaining and grumbling.

Do you enjoy being around a person who is always complaining?

Pray Today:

"Heavenly Father, help me live and act in a happy way because I know You love me and I want to please You in the things I do and say. Help me do my work without grumbling. Help me play with others without having to have my own way all the time. Forgive me for days when I have been a grouch. In Jesus' name I pray. Amen."

July 2

Read the Bible:

Find and read Matthew 5:44-47 in your Bible. Underline verse 44.

"But now I tell you: love your enemies, and pray for those who persecute you, so that you will become the sons of your Father in heaven. For he makes his sun to shine on bad and good people alike, and gives rain to those who do good and those who do evil. Why should God reward you, if you love only the people who love you? Even the tax collectors do that! And if you speak only to your friends, have you done anything out of the ordinary? Even the pagans do that!" (GNB).

Think About This:

Can you think of a person you have a hard time liking? It is easy to want to be with our friends and spend time with them. It is not so easy to be friendly or even speak to those who are unkind to us. What two things did Jesus say we should do for our enemies?

1.
2.

Can this Scripture help you decide how to treat people?

Pray Today:

Think of someone you do not like very much. Pray for that person. Say the person's name to God as you pray. If you see the person today, speak to them. Ask God to help you be the kind of friend you should be. Can you invite this person to your church?

July 3

Read the Bible:

Read and lightly color Deuteronomy 31:7-8.

Think About This:

When Joshua became the leader of the Israelites after Moses became old, Moses gave them some good advice. "The Lord your God himself will go before you" (Verse 3, GNB).

Moses knew that there would be people who would fight against Joshua and the Israelites. The verses for today are ones that Moses said to Joshua: "Be determined and confident; you are the one who will lead these people to occupy the land that the Lord promised to their ancestors. The Lord himself will lead you and be with you. He will not fail you or abandon you, so do not lose courage or be afraid" (GNB).

Knowing that God has promised to always be with you should help you when you feel lonely.

Pray Today:

"Heavenly Father, thank You for being with me. Help me remember that even when I am all alone, You are right there with me. Because I know that, help me do things that please You because I love You. In Jesus' name I pray. Amen."

July 4

Read the Bible:

Read and lightly color 1 Corinthians 6:19-20. "Or do you not know that your body is a temple of the Holy Spirit who is in you, whom you have from God, and that you are not your own? For you have been bought with a price: therefore glorify God in your body" (NASB).

Think About This:

We belong to God. When we become Christians, we ask Christ to come into our lives. We need to take care of our bodies. Look at the list below. Put an "N" by the things you should not put into your mind and body. Put a "Y" by the things that are good for your mind and body.

____ vegetables and fruits ____ alcohol ____ drugs ____ tobacco ____ exercise ____ dirty stories and jokes ____ good books ____ staying up late watching TV

Pray Today:

"Heavenly Father, I want to put good things into my mind and body. Help me say no to things that are not good. Help me choose the best things to eat that will make my body healthy. Help me want to dress and act in ways pleasing to You. Thank You for parents who help me in making good choices. Help me listen to them. In Jesus' name. Amen."

July 5

Read the Bible:

Read the story of an angry brother in Luke 15:11-32.
Locate and lightly color this verse found in Ephesians 4:26.

"Be angry, and yet do not sin; do not let the sun go down on your anger" (NASB).

Think About This:

What are some things that make you angry? What do you do to express your anger? You are getting old enough to learn to control your anger. God can help you deal with your anger in ways that do not hurt others. Look at the list of ways to handle anger. Mark through those you think are unacceptable for someone your age. Put a "T" by those you will try the next time you get angry.

- Kick and scream.
- Hit with your fists or some other object.
- Go off by yourself until you are calmer.
- Ask your parents what to do about your problem.
- Ask God to help you with your anger.
- Tell the person they are never to come to your home again—ever!
- Make peace with the one with whom you are angry. Say you are sorry. Pray for the person.

Pray Today:

Ask God to help you when you are angry.

July 6

Read the Bible:

Read and underline Proverbs 15:31-32.

"If you pay attention when you are corrected, you are wise. If you refuse to learn, you are hurting yourself. If you accept correction, you will become wiser" (GNB).

Think About This:

Dee Anna was always angry when her mom corrected her table manners. What did it matter how you hold your fork? Who cares if you slurp every once in a while? Dee Anna didn't really care what foods were OK to eat with fingers and which were not. Most of the time she would have liked to just eat in front of the TV.

At Terri's slumber party Dee Anna heard some of the girls talking about her table manners. She felt her face turn red.

Pray Today:

Ask God to help you know that grownups give advice and correct young people because they love them and do not want them to be embarrassed.

July 7

Read the Bible:

Lightly color Leviticus 19:16.
"Do not spread lies about anyone" (GNB).
Also lightly color Ephesians 4:25. "No more lying then! Everyone must tell the truth to his fellow believer, because we are all members together in the body of Christ" (GNB).

Think About This:

Why do we "add to a story" about a person? How do you feel when you know you have told something that is not true about a person?

Lying is a habit that usually hurts others. Try to think before you speak. Think about how you would like to be treated. Practice telling the truth. Your parents and friends will know then that when you say something, they can count on it being the truth.

Pray Today:

Ask for forgiveness if you remember any lies you have told. Ask God to help you practice telling the truth.

July 8

Read the Bible:

Can you find and lightly color Hebrews 10:24-25?

"Let us be concerned for one another, to help one another to show love and to do good. Let us not give up the habit of meeting together, as some are doing. Instead, let us encourage one another all the more, since you see that the Day of the Lord is coming nearer" (GNB).

Now find Luke 4:16. Color this verse, also.

Think About This:

The fourth chapter of Luke tells that Jesus "went as usual" to the synagogue. That means that Jesus had made a habit of attending the teaching and worship services of the synagogue. Can you name three reasons you go to church?

1.
2.
3.

Can these reasons help you decide to make church attendance an important part of your life?

Pray Today:

Thank God for your church. Thank Him that you can be with others to learn about Jesus. Thank Him for your church family. Ask God to help you enjoy going to church.

July 9

Read the Bible:

Read, lightly color, and think about Acts 20:35.
"I have shown you in all things that by working hard in this way we must help the weak, remembering the words that the Lord Jesus himself said, 'There is more happiness in giving than in receiving' " (GNB).

Think About This:

Finish this sentence: Being selfish is _____
_____
_____ .

Boys and girls, men and women are known by the way they act. How would you feel if you knew that people thought you were selfish? _____
_____ .

Have you ever given something to someone, or done something for someone and you felt happy inside and out? God is pleased when we are willing to give to others.

Pray Today:

"Heavenly Father, thank You for unselfishly giving Your Son, Jesus Christ. Help me be happy in sharing what I have and what I can do with others. In Jesus' name I pray. Amen."

July 10

Read the Bible:

Locate, read, and underline Deuteronomy 6:18 and also Romans 12:17.

"Never pay back evil for evil to anyone. Respect what is right in the sight of all men" (Romans 12:17, NASB).

Think About This:

Jeremy was proud of the hits he had gotten in the ball game. He had enjoyed hearing his family and friends cheer. By the time he remembered the social studies test, it was too late to study. He sat next to Brenda. Brenda always knew all the answers. Just this one time Jeremy thought he could lean over far enough to copy some of the answers. He knew that his teacher would be reading while the test was being taken. None of the other students would see him if he was careful.

Do you think Jeremy's family and friends would cheer him for making a good grade if they knew he had cheated?

Pray Today:

Ask God to help you choose to do the right and honest thing when you are tempted to cheat.

July 11

Read the Bible:

Locate Hebrews 13:6 and Isaiah 12:2. Lightly color these verses. "Let us be bold, then, and say, the Lord is my helper, I will not be afraid. What can anyone do to me?" (Hebrews 13:6, GNB).

"God is my savior; I will trust him and not be afraid. The Lord gives me power and strength: he is my savior" (Isaiah 12:2, GNB).

Think About This:

To whom do you talk when you feel sad? Do you talk to a friend? Do you talk to your mom or dad? Do you talk to a favorite Sunday School teacher?

It is OK to feel sad, but remember that God made you and He loves you.

Pray Today:

"Heavenly Father, sometimes I feel sad and sometimes I do not even know why I am sad. Help me look for reasons to be happy. Help me remember that You love me. In Jesus' name I pray. Amen."

July 12

Read the Bible:

Locate and read Psalm 46. Lightly color verses 1 through 3.

"God is our refuge and strength, an ever present help in trouble. Therefore we will not fear, though the earth give way and the mountains fall into the heart of the sea, though its waters roar and foam and the mountains quake with their surging" (NIV).

Think About This:

There are some scary times in our lives. What are some times you are afraid? Have you ever been in trouble? Did you feel upset when you did not know how things were going to turn out? Many times grownups feel the same way. Our strength comes from God. He is with us in every time of trouble.

Pray Today:

"Dear Father, sometimes I get in trouble and I am upset. Sometimes I do not know what to do. Help me remember these Bible verses and trust You. In Jesus' name I pray. Amen."

July 13

Read the Bible:

Locate and lightly color Matthew 4:10.

"Then Jesus answered, 'Go away, Satan! The scripture says, Worship the Lord your God and serve only him!' "

Think About This:

After Jesus was baptized, He went into the wilderness and was tempted by Satan. Satan came to Jesus when He was hungry and offered Him food. Then Satan offered Jesus popularity. A third time Satan offered an easy way to gain power. Jesus said no.

Jesus chose God's way. When are some times when you need to say no to Satan? Do you have friends who try to talk you into doing things you should not do? Tell them no!

Pray Today:

Ask God to help you be strong enough to say no to the people and things that try to draw you away from doing the things He wants you to do.

July 14

Read the Bible:

Read Matthew 6:9-15. Underline verse 12.

"Forgive us the wrongs we have done, as we forgive the wrongs that others have done to us" (GNB).

Think About This:

Michael was so mad at Megan he could not think about anything else! He was angry with her for riding his bike without asking. To make matters worse, she had scraped some of the paint off after he had been so careful how he parked his bike.

Megan had told Michael she was sorry. She reminded him of the time he tossed a ball and broke a little china doll Granny Hensley had given her.

"I forgave you, Michael," Megan said.

Pray Today:

"Heavenly Father, help me be ready to forgive others when they do things I do not like. Forgive me when I do not treat my family and friends the way You want me to. In Jesus' name I pray. Amen."

July 15

Read the Bible:

Locate and lightly color Philippians 4:13 in your Bible. Put your own name in the blank. "_____ can do all things through Christ which strengtheneth me."

Think About This:

The young people in the special education department wanted to do something for someone. All of the young people had a learning problem. They worked hard at learning some songs and Bible verses to share with a lonely older lady. Mrs. Annie cried when the young people finished singing and saying their Bible verses.

Probably any of you reading this could have learned the songs and Bible verses on one Sunday. The young people in the special education department believed Philippians 4:13. There is not a job too hard for you to do with God's help.

Pray Today:

Ask God to give you strength to do your best.

July 16

Read the Bible:

Read these verses from your Bible: Exodus 24:7; James 1:22; and 1 Samuel 15:22.

"And Samuel said, Hath the Lord as great delight in burnt offerings and sacrifices, as in obeying the voice of the Lord? Behold, to obey is better than sacrifice, and to hearken than the fat of rams" (1 Samuel 15:22).

Think About This:

The Bible teaches that we should obey. First of all, we are to obey God. We are to obey the teachings in the Bible. When the prophet Samuel talked to King Saul, he told the king that God wanted him to obey more than He wanted the king to offer many sacrifices of lambs.

Obeying God is one of the best ways of showing Him that you love Him. Obeying your parents is one of the best ways to show them that you love them.

Pray Today:

"Heavenly Father, sometimes I do not obey. Sometimes I do not want to obey. I know this is wrong. Please help me know that You want my obedience more than You want money or other gifts and sacrifices I might make. I love You and need Your help to be obedient. In Jesus' name I pray. Amen."

Elijah/Elisha

July 17

Read the Bible:

Read 1 Kings 17:1-6.

Locate and lightly color Philippians 4:19. "And my God will meet all your needs according to his glorious riches in Christ Jesus" (NIV).

Think About This:

God supplied food and water for His prophet, Elijah. Name five things you are thankful for that God has provided for you.

1.
2.
3.
4.
5.

Pray Today:

Thank God for the things He provides for you and your family. Thank Him for loving you.

July 18

Read the Bible:

Read 1 Kings 17:7-16. Lightly color Psalm 145:3.
"The Lord is great and is to be highly praised; his greatness is beyond understanding" (GNB).

Think about this:

What did the woman say to Elijah when he asked her to bring him food and water?

What did the woman say she and her son would do after they ate their last food?

When did Elijah tell the woman the jars of flour and oil would run out?

Did God do as Elijah said He would?

Pray Today:

Thank God for interesting stories in the Bible. Thank God that the Bible is true. Thank God for ways He shows His love.

July 19

Read the Bible:

Read 1 Kings 18:16-39.

Think About This:

This wonderful story is a favorite one about the prophet, Elijah. Name two things Elijah did to prove that God was the one true God. Wouldn't it have been exciting to have been on Mount Carmel that day?

Pray Today:

"Heavenly Father, help me trust You at all times. Thank You for the story of Elijah. In Jesus' name I pray. Amen."

July 20

Read the Bible:

Read 1 Kings 18:41-46. Underline verse 46.

Think About This:

When this story took place, it had not rained for several years. (Read 18:1.)

How many times did the servant go to look for a cloud in the sky? How big was the cloud that the servant finally saw in the far-off sky? Who arrived at Jezreel first, King Ahab or Elijah?

Pray Today:

Thank God for rain. Thank God for water and all the ways we use it.

July 21

Read the Bible:

Read 2 Kings 2:1-14.

Think About This:

Do you know a person that you would like to be like? Elisha was younger than his friend, Elijah. He loved God and wanted to serve Him just as Elijah was doing. Now it was time for Elijah to go to be with the Lord.

How did the men get across the Jordan River?

How did Elijah go to heaven?

Pray Today:

Thank God for parents and teachers who set a good example for you to follow.

July 22

Read the Bible:

Read 2 Kings 4:1-7.
Locate in the Bible and lightly color Psalm 145:19.
"He supplies the needs of those who honor him; he hears their cries and saves them" (GNB).

Think About This:

Does this story remind you of the one about Elijah?
Do you think Elisha is like Elijah? How can your family help another family who needs food?

Pray Today:

Pray that persons you help will understand more about God's love because of what you do.

July 23

Read the Bible:

Read 2 Kings 4:8-17.

Lightly color Psalm 95:6-7. "Come, let us bow down and worship him; let us kneel before the Lord our Maker! He is our God; we are the people he cares for, the flock for which he provides" (GNB).

Think About This:

Elisha looked for a way to show his thanks to the woman from Shunem. When someone does something special for you, how do you show your thanks? Check the things you can do to show your thanks to someone. _____ Pray for them. _____ Write a note. _____ Give a hug. _____ Help them with work they have to do.

Pray today:

"Heavenly Father, thank You for the many ways You show that You love me. Help me remember to be thankful to others who are helpful and kind to me. In Jesus' name I pray. Amen."

Names of Jesus

July 24

Read the Bible:

Locate these Bible verses to find the names for Jesus. Fill in the blanks. Underline the name for Jesus in each Bible verse.

- "And she shall bring forth a son, and thou shalt call his name _____: for he shall save his people from their sins" (Matthew 1:21).
- "And lo a voice from heaven, saying, This is my _____ ____, in whom I am well pleased" (Matthew 3:17).
- "And Simon Peter answered and said, Thou art the _____, the ____ ____ ____ _____" (Matthew 16: 16).

Think About This:

God told Mary and Joseph to name His Son, Jesus. He was called many names while He lived on earth. He is called many names today. Do you have a favorite name for Him?

Pray Today:

"Heavenly Father, thank You for giving us special names for Jesus. Help me always use His name and Your name in ways that please You. In Jesus' name I pray. Amen."

July 25

Read the Bible:

Locate Mark 10:17 and John 1:29 in your Bible. Fill in the missing words. Lightly color the words that are names for Jesus.

"And when he was gone forth into the way, there came one running, and kneeled to him, and asked him, _____ _____, what shall I do that I may inherit eternal life?" (Mark 10:17).

"For unto you is born this day in the city of David a _____, which is _____ the _____" (Luke 2:11).

"The next day John seeth Jesus coming unto him, and saith, Behold the _____ of _____, which taketh away the sin of the world" (John 1:29).

Think About This:

Any name given to Jesus should be used in a way that shows love and respect. One of the Ten Commandments tells us that we should not take the name of God in vain. That means that we are not to use His name carelessly or in cursing. Are you careful how you use a name for God or Jesus?

Pray Today:

Ask God to help you realize that names stand for something and that we should honor God by using His name in a way that honors Him.

July 26

Read the Bible:

Open your Bible to these Bible verses: John 12:13 and John 20:28. Underline the special names for Jesus.

Think About This:

A favorite name for Jesus is the Good Shepherd. Do you remember how David begins Psalm 23? "The Lord is my shepherd, I shall not want." Read the Psalm before you go to sleep tonight.

Pray Today:

"Heavenly Father, thank You for Psalm 23. Thank You for loving me. Help me love You enough to always try to obey You. I love You. In Jesus' name I pray. Amen."

July 27

Read the Bible:

The Old Testament has names for Jesus. Locate Isaiah 9:6. How many names are given for Jesus? Lightly color each name.

Think About This:

Many years before Jesus was born in Bethlehem, the prophet Isaiah said He would be born. Isaiah knew God's Son would be all that the names said He would be.

Pray Today:

"Heavenly Father, thank You for being wonderful to me. Thank You for being a mighty God. Thank You for being a Heavenly Father. Thank You for loving me. In Jesus' name I pray. Amen."

July 28

Read the Bible:

Read John 14:1-6. Underline verse 6.

"Jesus answered him, 'I am the way, the truth, and the life; no one goes to the Father except by me'" (GNB).

Think About This:

In this chapter, Jesus told people that those who believed in God should also believe in Him. He is preparing a place in heaven for those who trust in Him. When Thomas asked how to get to heaven, what did Jesus answer? "I am the _____, the _____, and the _____; no one goes to the Father except by me."

Pray Today:

Thank God for Jesus. Thank God for heaven.

July 29

Read the Bible:

Lightly color Luke 5:5; 1 Corinthians 10:4; and Matthew 2:4.

Think About This:

Everyone loved Emily. Emily was only two. The older children at her church enjoyed helping take care of her. They liked to ask her to tell them the pet names her relatives called her. Grandmother Hill called her Angel. Papa Hill called her his little Sweetheart. Uncle Bill called her Peanut, and Aunt Jane called her Sugar Pie. Though Emily was very young, she knew the names were spoken in love.

Pray Today:

"Heavenly Father, help me use names that are loving and kind when I speak to others. Help me be careful not to hurt others by the names I call them. In Jesus' name I pray. Amen."

July 30

Read the Bible:

Locate and lightly color the names given for Jesus in 1 Timothy 6:14-15.

Think About This:

Jesus is the "King of kings" and "Lord of Lords." What name for Jesus do you think is the most beautiful?
_____

What name for Jesus is the one you like best? ____

Pray Today:

Thank God for Jesus.

July 31

Read the Bible:

Lightly color Isaiah 7:14.

"Well then, the Lord himself will give you a sign: a young woman who is pregnant will have a son and will name him 'Immanuel'" (GNB).

Think About This:

There are many names for Jesus. In the word maze you will find some of those names. Can you find these names? Wonderful, Immanuel, Jesus, Teacher, Son, Savior, Counselor, Master, Shepherd, Way, Truth, Life, King, Lord, Christ, Friend, Redeemer.

J	C	O	U	N	S	E	L	O	R
X	H	T	U	R	T	L	Y	J	C
Y	R	J	O	X	L	Y	O	Z	A
K	I	N	G	C	O	Y	Q	R	Z
D	S	A	V	I	O	R	Y	X	D
N	T	X	Y	M	A	S	T	E	R
E	K	J	X	M	J	Z	K	X	E
I	Y	T	E	A	C	H	E	R	H
R	X	S	O	N	X	L	K	J	P
F	J	E	S	U	S	I	J	E	E
W	O	N	D	E	R	F	U	L	H
A	X	Z	Y	L	X	E	J	I	S
Y	Z	R	E	D	E	E	M	E	R

Pray Today:

Tell Jesus your favorite name for Him. Ask Him to help you always use His name in the right way.

Women of the Bible

August 1

Read the Bible:

Read part of the story of Esther in Esther 2:5-10 and 2:16-18. When you finish reading those verses, turn to and read 7:1-6.

Think About This:

Esther is known as "good queen Esther" because she spoke to the king about her people. Mordecai, her cousin, had been her adviser. Haman was a cruel, selfish man. Haman did not like Jewish people. He wanted them killed. God is never pleased when we "pick on" people who are different from us.

Pray Today:

Ask God to help you be a friend to all people. If there are people in your school or community who are of another nationality or who are in some way different from you, try to be a friend.

August 2

Read the Bible:

Read Judges 4:4-16 and 5:1-3. Underline 5:1-3.

Think About This:

Deborah was a prophet and served as a judge to help the people of Israel. She would sit under the shade of a palm tree and make decisions as she talked with the people. The Lord was with Deborah and helped her to be a wise judge.

One day Deborah sent for Barak. What did she want Barak to do? What happened? Who were the people in the story?

Pray Today:

Thank God for using women to help with His work. Do you know a lady who tells others of Jesus or who gives wise advice? Thank God for that person.

August 3

Read the Bible:

Read Luke 1:5-8. Also read Luke 1:39-56.

Think About This:

Elizabeth was a woman who loved and trusted God. She was a relative and a special friend to Mary, the mother of Jesus. Can you answer these questions about Elizabeth?

Who was Elizabeth's husband?

What did Elizabeth's husband do?

Why was Elizabeth surprised that she and Zechariah would have a son?

What did Elizabeth and Zechariah name their son?

Their son was later called "John the Baptist." He told people Jesus would come. Later he baptized Jesus.

Pray Today:

Thank God for the Bible. Thank Him for your family.

August 4

Read the Bible:

Read Luke 10:38-41.

Think About This:

How would you describe Martha?
She was _____ .
She liked to _____ .
She did not like _____ .
How would you describe Mary?
She was usually _____ .
She enjoyed _____ .

Do you have a sister or brother? How do you treat each other? Do you think God is pleased with the way you treat each other? What can you do to make your home a happier place?

Pray Today:

Ask God to help you treat your family just the way He wants you to. Ask Him to help you listen to those who teach about Jesus.

August 5

Read the Bible:

Find and read Acts 9:36-42.

"But rather give alms of such things as ye have" (Luke 11:41a).

Think About This:

Dorcas could sew. She made coats and other clothing for needy families. Sewing for others was something Dorcas could do to show she loved and served God.

Ken stayed thirty minutes each weekday morning with a retarded child while the child's mother drove the father to work.

Do you know how to do something that would be helpful to others? Could you help someone with math or English? Could you do yard work?

Pray Today:

Ask God to help you unselfishly share what you can do with others.

August 6

Read the Bible:

Read Acts 12:1-19 to find the story of Rhoda.

Think About This:

Rhoda was a young woman. She evidently was sent to answer Peter's knocking at the gate. Can you imagine how surprised she was to find Peter when she knew he was supposed to be chained in prison?

Have you ever been given instructions to do something that took courage? Remember that it was late at night when Rhoda went to the gate.

Ed Taylor, a missionary to migrant workers, tells about riding his horse at night when he was a child to get the doctor for his sick mother. Though he was frightened, he asked God to go with him.

Pray Today:

"Heavenly Father, help me follow instructions and do what my parents tell me to do. Help me always want to obey You. In Jesus' name I pray. Amen."

August 7

Read the Bible:

Read Acts 16:12-15 and then read verse 40 of that chapter. Read also Philippians 1:1-10.

Think About This:

Who was Lydia? What business was she in? Where was the prayer meeting that Paul visited? What happened after the teaching by Paul? How did Lydia help the missionaries?

Pray Today:

Lydia was generous and helpful to Paul and showed her love by doing for others. Pray that you will grow to be generous and helpful to God's missionaries.

August 8

Read the Bible:

Read about Priscilla in Acts 18:1-3 and 18:26. Find and read 1 Corinthians 16:19 and 2 Timothy 4:19.

Think About This:

Fill in the blanks with facts about Priscilla.

Priscilla was the wife of A _____.

Priscilla went with P_____ to _____ (Acts 18:18).

Priscilla and Aquila took A _____ home with them to teach him about Jesus (Acts 18:26).

Priscilla and Aquila had a c_____ meeting at their house (1 Corinthians 16:19).

Priscilla and Aquila were helpers. They were special friends to Paul. He remembered them with great joy.

Pray Today:

Ask God to help you be helpful to your pastor. You can help your Sunday School teacher by obeying and listening and helping others in your church.

Brothers

August 9

Read the Bible:

Read John 15:17 in your Bible.
"This is my command: Love each other" (NIV).

Think About This:

Cain and Abel were the first brothers in the Bible. The story of their family is in the Book of Genesis. Cain was angry with his brother. He did not control his anger. God is not pleased when we treat our brothers and sisters badly. Say the Bible verse that you read in John 15:17.

List three things you will do for people in your family that will show them that you love and care about them.

1.
2.
3.

Pray Today:

Pray for each member of your family. Call each one by name. Ask God to help you do your part to make a happy home.

August 10

Read the Bible:

Underline Matthew 6:14 in your Bible.

"If you forgive others the wrongs they have done to you, your Father in heaven will also forgive you. But if you do not forgive others, then your Father will not forgive the wrongs you have done" (GNB).

Think About This:

Jacob and Esau were brothers. Jacob tricked Esau when they were both living at home. Esau said that one day he would kill his brother. Read in Genesis 33:3-4 what happened when the two brothers finally met.

How does it feel when someone forgives you? How does it feel to forgive someone else?

Pray today:

Ask God to help you to treat your family as you should. Ask God to help you be forgiving and to be big enough to ask forgiveness of family members you have offended in some way.

August 11

Read the Bible:

Locate, read, and lightly color Matthew 5:16.

"In the same way your light must shine before people, so that they will see the good things you do and praise your Father in heaven" (GNB).

Think About This:

Joseph had eleven brothers. His younger brother was Benjamin. Joseph had some problems with his brothers as he was growing to be a man. When his brothers were angry and sold him, he was taken to Egypt. It was here that Joseph became second to the king. When his brothers came for grain, Joseph treated them just as the Bible verse you read in Matthew 5:16. Read the verse once more. What does the verse tell you about how you should act?

Pray Today:

Ask God to help you when you feel like bragging about the things you have done. Thank Him for talents He has given you. Ask God to help you "let your light shine" so people will see by your actions that you love Christ.

August 12

Read the Bible:

Read John 1:35-42. Luke 6:31 is a good Bible verse that tells us how to treat others.

"Do for others just what you want them to do for you" (GNB).

Think About This:

Why did Andrew want his brother to meet Jesus? Name two people you will invite to your church.

1.
2.

Pray Today:

If you have a brother or sister, thank God especially for them today. Ask God to help you share what you know about Jesus with your family.

August 13

Read the Bible:

Read Matthew 4:18-22. Underline verse 19. " 'Come, follow me,' Jesus said, 'and I will make you fishers of men' " (NIV).

Think About This:

Name the two sets of brothers that Jesus called to be His disciples.

_____ and _____

_____ and _____.

Do you know anyone that God has called to work for Him? Remember that God wants you to serve Him whether you are an engineer, a nurse, a teacher, or have some other job.

Pray Today:

"Heavenly Father, help me know what work I should do. Help me love and serve You all of my life. In Jesus' name I pray. Amen."

August 14

Read the Bible:

Read John 15:12-14.

"My commandment is this: love one another, just as I love you" (verse 12, GNB).

Think About This:

David had seven brothers. He was the youngest son. Perhaps his brothers were enough older that they did not spend much time with him. King Saul's son, Jonathan, was like a brother to David.

Brothers grow to care about each other. They want to help and protect each other. They like to give presents to each other.

Pray Today:

If you have a brother, a sister, or a good friend who is like a brother or sister, thank God for that person.

August 15

Read the Bible:

Find a story of Aaron and Moses in Exodus 3:1-11 and 4:1-17.

Underline Psalm 133:1 in your Bible.

"How wonderful it is, how pleasant, for God's people to live together in harmony!" (Psalm 133:1, GNB).

Think About This:

What did God have for Moses to do?

What was Moses' response and excuse?

Who did God say could speak for Moses?

God had a job for Moses to do and Aaron, Moses' brother, was to help get the job done.

Pray Today:

Thank God for giving helpers when there is a hard job to do and you do not feel like you can do it by yourself. If you have a brother or sister, pray especially for them today.

Promises

August 16

Read the Bible:

Underline Psalm 86:5 in your Bible.

Think About This:

How does it feel when you ask someone to forgive you and they refuse to—even when you say you are sorry?

Isn't it wonderful to know that God is always ready to forgive us? All we have to do is ask Him.

Pray Today:

Ask God to help you remember anything you have done today that you need to ask forgiveness for. Tell God that you are sorry. Thank Him for forgiving you. Ask Him to help you not to make the same mistakes. Thank Him for the promise He made in Psalm 86:5.

August 17

Read the Bible:

Read and underline Matthew 28:20 in your Bible.

Think About This:

This promise from Jesus is that He will be with you forever. Good times and bad times; sick times and well times; happy times and sad times; God will always be with you.

Pray Today:

Say thank You to God for promises made and promises kept. Thank Him for being with you all twenty-four hours of the day.

August 18

Read the Bible:

Underline this verse found in Psalm 4:8 in your Bible.
"When I lie down, I go to sleep in peace; you alone,
O Lord, keep me perfectly safe" (GNB).

Think About This:

Have you ever been afraid at night? Darylene was.
She and her family had moved far from her friends. She
heard all kinds of strange noises in their two-story
house. Her mom helped her find Psalm 4:8 in her Bible.
Together they memorized the verse. Saying the verse
over and over helped Darylene learn to believe the
verse and to trust God to take away her fear.

Pray Today:

Say the Bible verse for today as a prayer.

August 19

Read the Bible:

Locate and read Genesis 8:17-22 and 9:8-17.

Think About This:

After the Flood, Noah and his family came out of the ark and built an altar to worship God. God made a covenant (an agreement or promise) to Noah. What were the promises God made?

Genesis 8:21-22 _____

_____

Genesis 9:8-17 _____

_____

Are these promises still in effect today? Does God still keep His promises to us?

Pray Today:

"Dear Heavenly Father, thank You for keeping Your promises to me. I know I can always count on You. In Jesus' name. Amen."

August 20

Read the Bible:

Find and lightly color Psalm 16:11.

"You will show me the path that leads to life; your presence fills me with joy and brings me pleasure forever" (GNB).

Think About This:

Joy is another word for happiness. The Bible tells you how to become a Christian. There are verses that tell you how to treat others. There are verses that tell you how to behave. Knowing that God is with you should bring you happiness or joy.

Can you softly sing "Joy to the World"?

Pray Today:

Thank God for the joy of knowing that He is with you wherever you are.

August 21

Read the Bible:

Read 2 Samuel 9:1-13.

"Our purpose is to do what is right, not only in the sight of the Lord, but in the sight of man" (2 Corinthians 8:21, GNB).

Underline 2 Corinthians 8:21 in your Bible.

Think About This:

Making a promise is easier than keeping a promise. Probably only God knew that David had made a promise to his friend Jonathan. David wanted both God and others to know that when he made a promise, he tried to keep that promise.

Pray Today:

Ask God to help you remember to treat people the way you would like to be treated.

August 22

Read the Bible:

Locate and underline Psalm 28:7.

"The Lord protects and defends me; I trust in him. He gives me help and makes me glad; I praise him with joyful songs" (GNB).

Think About This:

When Bethany went to the hospital, she remembered what her mother told her. "Trust God to take care of you. He will protect you."

Bethany looked out the hospital window. Most of the windows in the homes were dark. She remembered a Bible verse that said God did not sleep. She opened her Bible to Psalm 121:3 and read the verse. As she looked out over the quiet streets she began to sing quietly, "I am so glad that Jesus loves me, Jesus loves me, Jesus loves me. . . ." Someone else was singing! Bethany turned. The night nurse was smiling. "We've got a busy day tomorrow, Bethany. Let's get you in bed!"

Pray Today:

"Heavenly Father, thank You for watching over me at times when I need to trust You. Thank You for Bible verses and songs that remind us of Your love. In Jesus' name. Amen."

August 23

Read the Bible:

Find and lightly color Luke 15:7.

Think About This:

This wonderful Bible verse tells us that there is joy in heaven when a person is sorry for sin and chooses Jesus as his Savior! Have you caused joy in heaven by asking Jesus to come into your life?

Pray Today:

Thank God for times of joy. Thank Him for getting heaven ready for those who trust Jesus as their Savior.

Disciples

August 24

Read the Bible:

Read about John, the disciple. He wrote about God's love in 1 John 4:1-12. Underline verse 10.

"This is what love is: it is not that we have loved God, but that he loved us and sent his Son to be the means by which our sins are forgiven" (GNB).

Think About This:

• John was the brother of James.
• His father was named Zebedee.
• He stood at the cross when Jesus was crucified.
• Jesus told him to take Mary, His mother, home with him to care for her.
• He wrote the Gospel of John and the Book of Revelation. Three Epistles, 1, 2, and 3 John are also thought to be written by John.

Can you add other facts about John? What work did he do before he became a disciple? (Matthew 4:21-22).

Pray Today:

Thank God for people in the Bible like John from whom we learn about Jesus' love.

August 25

Read the Bible:

Read about Andrew, a fisherman, in Mark 1:16-18; Matthew 4:18-20; and John 6:1-13.

Think About This:

Who did Andrew bring to Jesus in John 6:1-13? Tell the story of the lad and his lunch to a member of your family. Shut your eyes and think about the events of the story. Wouldn't it have been exciting to have been there that day? How would you have felt if you had been the one with the lunch?

Pray Today:

"Heavenly Father, help me be willing to give You whatever I have. Help me use my life in some way to serve You. In Jesus' name. Amen."

August 26

Read the Bible:

Read about Peter, a disciple who made a mistake but who loved and served Jesus. Read the Scriptures passages to find the answers to the questions.

Think About This:

1. What name did Jesus give Peter? (Matthew 16:17).
2. What unusual experience convinced Peter that Jesus was truly the Son of God? (Luke 5:5-11).
3. Why were Peter and John arrested in Jerusalem? (Acts 4:1-2).
4. When did Peter deny Jesus and how was he reminded? (Luke 22:31-34 and Luke 22:54-60).

Pray Today:

"Dear God, help me be strong in my faith and not deny that I love You by the things I say and do. In Jesus' name I pray. Amen."

August 27

Read the Bible:

Read about Thomas, the disciple who doubted. Find John 20:24-29. Underline verse 29.

"Jesus said to him, 'Do you believe because you see me? How happy are those who believe without seeing me!'" (GNB).

Think About This:

What does the word, *doubt* mean? _____ .

Have you ever doubted someone or doubted whether something was true?

What did Thomas doubt?

Do you think Thomas later in his life doubted Jesus.

Pray Today:

"Dear God, help me not doubt Your love for me. Help me know that I am important to You. In Jesus' name I pray. Amen."

August 28

Read the Bible:

Read about Philip, a disciple who cared. Read John 1:43-47 and John 14:1-14. Underline verse 12.

Think About This:

Discover these facts about Philip:
- Jesus found Philip in the country of _____. (John 1:43)
- Philip's hometown was _____. (John 1:44)
- _____ was a friend of Philip. (John 1:45)
- Jesus promised His disciples that He would come _____ for them. (John 14:3)
- Philip asked Jesus to show him the _____. (John 14:8)

Pray Today:

Make a list of people you know that show by their lives that they care for others. Ask God to help you become a caring person.

August 29

Read the Bible:

Read about Matthew, the disciple who became a changed man. Read Luke 5:27-32. Underline or lightly color verses 31-32.

Think About This:

Answer these questions about Matthew.

• What is another name given for Matthew? (Luke 5:27)

• What was Matthew's work before he became a disciple? (Luke 5:27)

• What was Matthew's response when Jesus came to his office? (Luke 5:28)

• What kind of people were Matthew's old friends? (Luke 5:29-30)

• Who else came to the party Matthew gave? (Luke 5:29-30)

• What did Jesus answer when He was asked why He ate with tax collectors and sinners? (Luke 5:31-32)

Pray Today:

Thank God that He can change lives. Thank Him for being able to make dishonest people want to be honest. Thank Him for loving bad people and helping them to want to be good.

August 30

Read the Bible:

Read about Judas, the disciple who betrayed Jesus in John 13:2-3, 21-30; Matthew 26:14-16, 47-56; 27:3-5, 6-10.

Think About This:

What price was paid Judas for the betrayal? (Matthew 26:14-16)

_____

What did Judas do to show the enemy which person was Jesus? (Matthew 26:47-50)

_____

What did Judas do to try to make up for what he had done? (Matthew 27:3-5)

_____

What was done with the silver coins Judas had been given? (Matthew 27:6-10)

_____

Pray Today:

Pray that God will make you wise enough to know that following Jesus is the best way to live.

August 31

Read the Bible:

Read Matthew 10:1-4 and Mark 1:16-17. Lightly color the names of the disciples.

Think About This:

Make a list of all of the disciples.

Make a puppet of one of the disciples. Use paper plates, sacks, or anything you have used to make a puppet. Write a "Who am I?" riddle to go with the puppet. Share the puppet and riddle with others in your family.

Pray Today:

"Heavenly Father, help me be a follower of Jesus Christ. Help me do good things for people in Your name because I love You. In Jesus' name I pray. Amen."

Paul

September 1

Read the Bible:

Read about Saul, as a young man. Read Acts 21:39 and Acts 22:3 and 22:27-29.

Think About This:

Paul, the missionary, was first called Saul. Discover the answers to these facts about Saul as you read the verses again.

Saul was born in T_____, a city in C_____.

Saul was a J_____, but also a R_____.

He was a student of G_____ and lived in a large city called J_____.

Saul was a good student. He knew several languages. He lived in Jesus' time but he had not yet learned that Jesus of Nazareth was the promised Messiah. Acts 22:6-10 tells about the time he discovered that Jesus was God's Son, sent to be the Savior of the world.

Pray Today:

Thank God for men like Saul who allowed God to use them.

September 2

Read the Bible:

Read about Saul, the Persecutor. Read Acts 7:54-60. Also read Acts 8:1-3; 9:1-2; and 22:4-5.

Think About This:

How did Saul feel about the Christians?

Stephen was one of seven special workers chosen to help the disciples. What did Saul do while Stephen was being stoned?

What did Saul do when he found Christians?

Saul persecuted the Christians who told others about Jesus. He felt that Jesus could not be the Messiah or he would not have let himself be killed on the cross. Jesus' friends said that Jesus had risen from the dead.

Pray Today:

Ask God to help you understand how He could love Saul when he was so cruel to others who loved Jesus. Thank Him for loving you—even when you are cruel or mean.

September 3

Read the Bible:

Read about Saul, the believer. Read Acts 9:3-31. Underline verse 22.

Think About This:

Write a story or play about the experiences of Saul as a believer. Include people, places, and events.
Use these headings to make a list.

People   Places   Events

Pray Today:

Thank God that knowing Jesus can make a difference in our lives—even as it did in Saul's life.

September 4

Read the Bible:

Read about Saul, the assistant. Read Acts 11:22-30.

Think About This:

Whose assistant was Saul during this time?

What did Saul do?

Where were people first called Christians?

What is meant by the word *Christian?*

Are you a Christian?

Pray Today:

Pray for God to help you understand what it means to be a Christian. Do you need to talk to your parents or your pastor?

September 5

Read the Bible:

Read about Paul, the missionary. Read Acts 13:1-12. Lightly color the places Paul visited.

Think About This:

Where did Paul go on his first missionary journey?

Who went with him?

Was Barnabas really the first missionary because he was a friend and believed in Paul?

Look in the back of a Bible to find a map of Paul's missionary journeys.

Pray Today:

Ask God to help you be like Paul today and tell someone about Jesus.

September 6

Read the Bible:

Read Acts 16:11-15, 20-34. Underline verse 34.

Think About This:

Paul met with Lydia and her friends. He told them about Jesus. Wherever Paul was, he told people about Jesus.

What happened to the jailer and his family?

Why do you think Paul told so many people about Jesus?

How many people have you told about Jesus?

Pray Today:

"Heavenly Father, please help me share what I know about You with others. I want my friends and family to be Christians. Help me be a good witness. In Jesus' name I pray. Amen."

September 7

Read the Bible:

Read about Paul, a witness. Read Acts 26:1-32. Underline verse 22.

Think About This:

Have you ever told anyone about Jesus? Did they listen to you? What did the person do? What do you know that you could tell a person about Jesus?

1. Jesus is _____ .
2. Jesus taught us _____

_____ .

3. John 3:16 says: _____

_____ .

Pray Today:

Pray for someone you know who does not go to church and perhaps does not know about Jesus. Ask God for courage to tell the person about Jesus.

September 8

Read the Bible:

Read about Paul, the prisoner. Read Acts 28:16-30.

Think About This:

Paul was put in prison many times. He was beaten and sometimes left for dead. Did being treated so badly keep Paul from telling about Jesus? No!

What keeps you from telling others about Jesus?

____shyness

____not knowing what to say

____not caring about others

____too scared

____afraid the person will get mad

Pray Today:

"Dear God, help me be brave and tell others what I know about You. Help me watch what I say and what I do so that others will know that I love You. In Jesus' name I pray. Amen."

Work

September 9

Read the Bible:

Read in your Bible and lightly underline 2 Thessalonians 3:11-12.

"We say this because we hear that there are some people among you who live lazy lives and who do nothing except meddle in other people's business. In the name of the Lord Jesus Christ we command these people and warn them to lead orderly lives and work to earn their own living" (GNB).

Think about this:

What does the word *lazy* mean? What do people do when they are lazy. Have you ever been lazy when you had work to do?

How does it make you feel when you are just sitting around and others around you are doing all the work? How does it make you feel when you are doing all the work and others are just sitting around?

Pray Today:

Ask God to help you be a good worker and to do your part of the work without fussing.

September 10

Read the Bible:

Highlight Colossians 3:23 in your Bible.

"Whatever you do, work at it with all your heart, as though you were working for the Lord and not for men" (GNB).

Think About This:

Make a list of the work you are asked to do:

at home   at church

_____   _____

_____   _____

_____   _____

at school   other

_____   _____

_____   _____

_____   _____

How do you feel about work? What work do you enjoy doing? What work do you not like to do? How can you improve your attitude about work and your work habits?

Pray Today:

"Dear Father, help me know that everyone must work. I need to develop a good attitude about my work. In Jesus' name. Amen."

September 11

Read the Bible:

Find 1 Thessalonians 4:11 in your Bible.

"And to make it your ambition to lead a quiet life and attend to your own business and work with your hands, just as we commanded you" (NASB).

Think About This:

What are some good work habits? Add to the list below. Check the ones that you need to work on.

_____Be on time.

_____Be neat.

_____Do your best.

_____Follow instructions.

_____Do not waste material.

_____Do not waste time.

_____Cooperate with others.

_____

_____

Pray Today:

Ask God to help you develop good work habits, especially as you work on those you checked.

September 12

Read the Bible:

Can you say Proverbs 20:11 by memory? It begins "Even a child. . . ." Find the verse in your Bible to see if you said it correctly.

Think About This:

God uses many kinds of people to accomplish His work. Below is a list of familiar Bible people. Match the people with their work. The answers are in parentheses. Cover the answers with a sheet of paper and then check your answers.

(3) Matthew   1. herdsman
(4) Luke   2. shepherd
(5) Peter   3. tax collector
(1) Amos   4. doctor
(6) Paul   5. fisherman
(2) David   6. tentmaker
(7) Job   7. nobleman

Can children also be good workers and do important work? How can you help God with His work?

Pray Today:

Ask God to help you know what work you can do well.

September 13

Read the Bible:

Read these verses that tell some things the Old Testament teaches about work.
Ecclesiastes 9:10a
Ecclesiastes 10:18
Isaiah 1:17
Proverbs 6:6-11
Proverbs 3:5-6

Think About This:

Choose several words from the Scripture verses that would make a good work motto. Make a wall hanging to put in your room by writing a word or phrase on a large sheet of paper. Then decorate the borders around the word.

Pray Today:

Ask God to help you develop better attitudes about work.

September 14

Read the Bible:

Read each of the Scripture passages that tell some things the New Testament says about work.

1 Corinthians 3:9   Galatians 6:4-7
John 9:4   Ephesians 4:28

Think About This:

Write some words about work found in these verses.
Circle two verses you will try to memorize today.
Write a thank-you letter to someone who does work to help you.

Pray Today:

Ask God to help you be a good worker in your tasks today.

September 15

Read the Bible:

"Everything must be done in a proper and orderly way" (1 Corinthians 14:40, GNB).

Find this verse in your Bible and underline it.

Think About This:

God planned for people to work. What do you picture when you think about God putting Adam and Eve in the Garden of Eden? Can you see Adam and Eve busy or lazy; working or lying around?

In order to take care of the garden and animals Adam and Eve had to work. God planned in all His wisdom for people to get work done in a proper and orderly way.

Pray Today:

Write out a prayer asking God to guide you in choosing the right attitudes in your jobs at school, at church, and at home.

September 16

Read the Bible:

Underline lightly Ephesians 6:7-8.

"Serve wholeheartly, as if you were serving the Lord, not men, because you know that the Lord will reward everyone for whatever good he does, whether he is slave or free" (NIV).

Think About This:

How can you start finding out what God's plan is for your life's work? Does He let others help you?

God asks you to do things that you can do well. Each of us can serve the Lord with our whole hearts whatever we do.

Pray Today:

"Dear God, Help me serve You each day no matter what job I am doing. Help me stay close to You. In Jesus' name, Amen."

Stewardship

September 17

Read your Bible:

Read and highlight in your Bible James 1:17 and Psalm 24:1.

"Every good gift and every perfect gift is from above, and cometh down from the Father of lights" (James 1:17).

"The world and all that is in it belong to the Lord; the earth and all who live on it are his" (Psalm 24:1, GNB).

Think About This:

All that we have and are belongs to God. We are the managers, the keepers, the caretakers. We are trusted to do our best with our possessions, our time, and our talents. All things are to be used in ways that are pleasing to Him.

Pray Today:

Thank God for all the good things He has given you. Ask Him to help you be a good manager or steward.

September 18

Read the Bible:

Highlight Malachi 3:10 and 1 Corinthians 16:2 in your Bible.

"Bring the full amount of your tithes to the Temple, so that there will be plenty of food there. Put me to the test and you will see that I will open the windows of heaven and pour out on you in abundance all good things" (Malachi 3:10). "Every Sunday each of you must put aside some money, in proportion to what he has earned" (1 Corinthians 16:2*a*, GNB).

Think About This:

God knew that His people needed money to tell others about Jesus and to carry on the other work of the churches. His plan was for people to bring a tithe upon the first day of the week as they came to worship.

What is a tithe? It is a tenth of what you have earned. If you earned $1.00, what would your tithe be?

This is God's plan to support His work as we worship and show our love to Him.

Pray Today:

"Dear Heavenly Father, You know what is the best way to do things. You have taught us how to give. Help me develop good attitudes and habits about giving. In Jesus' name. Amen."

September 19

Read the Bible:

Find and read 2 Corinthians 8:5 and 1 Corinthians 4:2.

"It was more than we could have hoped for! First they gave themselves to the Lord; and then, by God's will they gave themselves to us as well" (2 Corinthians 8:5, GNB).

"Now it is required that those who have been given a trust must prove faithful" (1 Corinthians 4:2, NIV).

Think About This:

Early Christians first gave themselves to God and then in service of helping others. What do you have that God can use? Stewardship is not just for adults. It is for boys and girls, too.

Christian stewardship goes beyond possessions. It applies to how you spend your time and how you develop and use your talents.

Pray Today:

Ask God to help you be willing to be a good and faithful steward or manager of all that God has given you.

September 20

Read your Bible:

Highlight 2 Corinthians 9:7 in your Bible.
"Each one should give, then, as he has decided, not with regret or out of a sense of duty; for God loves the one who gives gladly" (GNB).

Think About This:

Our attitude about giving is very important. Match Scripture passages with attitudes toward money and other possessions. The words may go with more than one Scripture reference.

1 Kings 21:1-4	covetous
Matthew 25:34-36, 40	thrifty
Luke 10:30,33-35	greedy
Luke 12:16-20	generous
Luke 15:11-16	selfish
Luke 16:19-21	stingy
	generous
	charitable

Pray Today:

Ask God to help you be a cheerful giver.

September 21

Read the Bible:

Read and underline in your Bible 1 Timothy 4:14.
"Do not neglect the spiritual gift that is in you, which was given to you when the prophets spoke and the elders laid their hands on you" (GNB).

Think About This:

God gives talents, skills, and gifts for us to develop and use to help others and to serve Him.

What can you do well? Make a list.

Pray today:

"Our Father, thank You for many special gifts that You have given me. Help me develop my skills, learn well, and do my very best. In His name I pray. Amen."

September 22

Read the Bible:

"For the love of money is a source of all kinds of evil. Some have been so eager to have it that they have wandered away from the faith and have broken their hearts with many sorrows" (1 Timothy 6:10, GNB).

Underline this verse in your Bible.

Think About This:

How do you get money? Do you get an allowance? Do you work for your money? Do you ask your parents for money? Have you ever gotten money dishonestly? Have you ever taken money from someone smaller than you?

People who spend all their time thinking about money cause problems for themselves. The love of money can get you in big trouble.

Pray Today:

Ask God to help you have right feelings about money.

September 23

Read the Bible:

Read the story in Mark 12:41-44 of the widow who gave her money.

Think About This:

Many people gave money on this day but Jesus said the widow's gift was the greatest. She did not have much to give and, yet, she gave. God does not measure the amount of the gift but the attitude and love of the giver.

Draw a picture on a sheet of paper of the widow giving her coins. Your Bible may have a picture of the widow.

Pray Today:

Ask God to help you have the right attitude about giving your offering to your church.

September 24

Read the Bible:

Use your Bible to find the verses in the puzzle.

Think About This:

ACROSS

6. This word means management.

7. Time can be divided into d____. (Psalm 90:12)

10. One tenth of a person's possessions.(Leviticus 27:30)

12. God expects stewards to be f____. (1 Corinthians 4:2)

14. This feeling about money is the start of all kinds of evil.(1 Timothy 6:10)

16. Each person has the same amount of t____.

17. God owns the whole e____ and everything in it.(Psalm 24:1)

18. God's people are to bring these to His house.(Malachi 3:10)

DOWN

1. Christians are to give their offering on this day of the week.(1 Corinthians 16:2)

2. Early Christians first g____ themselves.(2 Corinthians 8:5)

3. Everything belongs to Him.

4. God loves a cheerful g____. (2 Corinthians 9:7)

5. We belong to God because He m____ us.(Psalm 100:3)

8. This belongs to God, too, for He made it.(Psalm 95:5)

9. All these good things come from God.(James 1:17)

10. Abilities that God gives each person, although not everyone has the same.

11. A person who takes care of something that belongs to someone else.(Luke 12:42)

13. The love of this is the beginning of all kinds of wrong. (1 Timothy 6:10)

15. God gives a person the power to earn this.(Deuteronomy 8:18)

Answers: stewardship, days, tithe, faithful, love, time, earth, tithes, first, gave, God, giver, made, sea, gifts, talents, steward, money, and wealth.

Pray Today:

Ask God to help you be a good steward.

Wisdom

September 25

Read the Bible:

Read Psalm 119:33-36. Lightly color the verses.
"Teach me, Lord, the meaning of your laws, and I will obey them at all times" (GNB).

Think About This:

How does a person get wisdom? Can you fill in these blanks?
- I can listen to _____ .
- I can read _____ .
- I can do my best at _____ to learn from my teachers.

Pray Today:

Thank God that He has allowed you to be able to think and use your mind. Ask Him to help you understand what the Bible teaches.

September 26

Read the Bible:

Locate and color Job 28:28.

"God said to men, 'To be wise, you must have reverence for the Lord. To understand, you must turn from evil' " (GNB).

Think About This:

What two things did God say were necessary for a person to be wise?

1.

2.

Circle the statements that you think show reverence to God.

• Sitting quietly while someone prays.

• Writing notes to your friend during the worship services.

• Laughing and talking when the Lord's Supper is being served.

• Thinking about the words to a hymn as you sing.

Read Job 28:28 one more time. Can you choose good things that will help you to be wise?

Pray Today:

"Heavenly Father, help me love You enough to be reverent. Help me love You enough to choose to do good. Help me not be talked into doing bad and help me not talk others into doing wrong. In Jesus' name I pray. Amen."

September 27

Read the Bible:

Read Daniel 2:16-23. Underline verses 20 through 23.

"God is wise and powerful! Praise him forever and ever. He controls the times and the seasons; he makes and unmakes kings; it is he who gives wisdom and understanding" (verses 20-21, GNB).

Think About This:

Daniel had just learned that the king was going to kill all the royal advisers in Babylon. That would mean that Daniel and his friends would also be killed. Daniel was wise enough to ask his friends to pray with him. These verses are a praise prayer that Daniel said in thanksgiving.

Pray Today:

Thank God for at least five things.

September 28

Read the Bible:

Read Luke 6:46-49. Locate and lightly color James 1:5.

"But if any of you lacks wisdom, he should pray to God, who will give it to him; because God gives generously and graciously to all" (GNB).

Think About This:

Being wise means more than listening. It means putting into practice the teachings of the Bible. What is a teaching from the Bible that you will try to put into practice this week?

Pray Today:

Is there something that is hard for you to learn? Ask God for wisdom. (He may help you realize that you need to do more study for some subjects!)

September 29

Read the Bible:

Read and lightly color Psalm 90:12.
"Teach us how short our life is, so that we may become wise" (GNB).

Think About This:

Even if we live 100 years, is that enough? Do we know how long we will live? One day, each person will stand before God and "give an account" of his life to God. This means that each person will have to tell God what he did with his time on earth. We need to begin serving God while we are young. A wise person can be ten, thirty-five, or sixty . . . there is no certain age. A person can be any of those ages and be very foolish and leave God out of his life!

Pray Today:

"Heavenly Father, I do not know how long I will live. Help me choose to please You while I am young. Help me serve You all of my life. In Jesus' name I pray. Amen."

September 30

Read the Bible:

Locate and underline or lightly color Proverbs 3:5-7.

"Trust in the Lord with all your heart. Never rely on what you think you know. Remember the Lord in everything you do, and he will show you the right way. Never let yourself think that you are wiser than you are; simply obey the Lord and refuse to do wrong" (GNB).

Think About This:

Make the Bible verse more personal by reading it aloud in this way:

"I will trust in the Lord with all my heart. I will not rely on what I think I know. I will remember the Lord in everything I do, and He will show me the right way. I will not think that I am wiser than I am; I will simply obey the Lord and I will refuse to do wrong."

Pray Today:

"Heavenly Father, I want to do the things those verses say. Thank You for the wise advice. In Jesus' name I pray. Amen."